ORTON GILLINGHAM SPELLING WORKBOOK

100 activities to help kids with dyslexia practice spelling

VOLUME 1

TERESA WILLOUGHBY

Introduction

Many common words sometimes have difficult pronunciations. This means that the child may have a difficult time reading and spelling them correctly. Some educators find that the best way of learning is by constantly rereading the words until the child has memorized them; however, the child usually tends to forget them.

The best way to teach high-frequency words is to use a multisensory method that will allow the child to see, hear and say the different words. In this book, you will find various activities focused on these types of words.

A good way to learn them is as follows.

1) You, as the educator, must choose the different graphemes, for example "th". Make sure that the child understands that this grapheme has two sounds.

2) Have the child carry out the exercises contained in this book related to the grapheme previously seen.

3) Get creative with the exercises in this book. For example, have the child write the different letters of each word that they find in large, cut them into squares, order them and read them out loud.

4) To complement the tasks contained in this book, the teacher can dictate a short phrase or different words that contain graphemes so that the child becomes familiar with the different sounds.

SPELLING LIST

These are the words that the students will practice in this volume.

are

call

eating

game

house

hope

made

only

love

nut

Alphabetical kites

Write each word in ABC order on the given kites.

are	eating	house	made	love
call	game	hope	only	nut

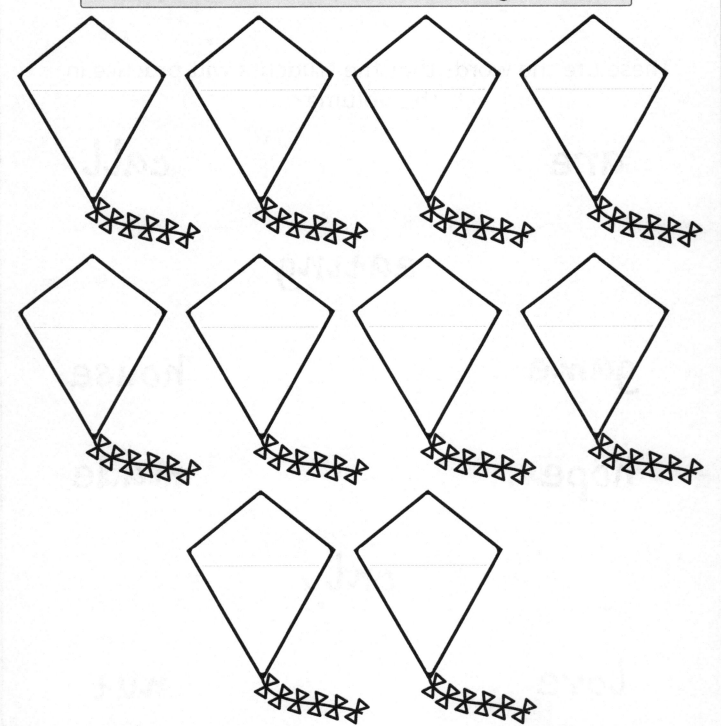

MAGIC Spelling Words

Write each word with white crayon and color over with marker to watch it "magically" appear.

are	eating	house	made	love
call	game	hope	only	nut

Secret code spelling words
Use the picture code to spell each of your words.

A ✈	H 🎩	O 🍊	V 🚐
B 🔔	I 🧁	P ✏	W ⌚
C 🧢	J 🍯	Q 🐦	X 👤
D 🐬	K 🪁	R 🐭	Y 🐂
E 🐘	L 🍃	S 🍓	Z 🦓
F 🐠	M 🌙	T 🚂	
G 🦒	N 🌰	U ☂	

1.- ✈ 🐭 🐘

_____

6.- 🎩 🍊 ✏ 🐘

_____

2.- 🌰 ☂ 🚂

_____

7.- 🧢 ✈ 🍃 🍃

_____

3.- 🐘 ✈ 🚂 🧁 🌰 🦒

_____

8.- 🦒 ✈ 🌙 🐘

_____

4.- 🎩 🍊 ☂ 🍓 🐘

_____

9.- 🍊 🌰 🍃 🐂

_____

5.- 🍃 🍊 🚐 🐘

_____

10.- 🌙 ✈ 🐬 🐘

_____

How many sounds?

Write the number of sounds in each of your spelling words.

	spelling word	sounds
1.-	are	1 2 3 4 5
2.-	call	1 2 3 4 5
3.-	eating	1 2 3 4 5
4.-	game	1 2 3 4 5
5.-	house	1 2 3 4 5
6.-	hope	1 2 3 4 5
7.-	made	1 2 3 4 5
8.-	only	1 2 3 4 5
9.-	love	1 2 3 4 5
10.-	nut	1 2 3 4 5

Sign language spelling

Sign each of your spelling words. Mark them off as you go.

are	☐	hope	☐
call	☐	made	☐
eating	☐	only	☐
game	☐	love	☐
house	☐	nut	☐

 # Roll a spelling word

Roll the dice then follow the directions for the number you rolled and complete the given task.

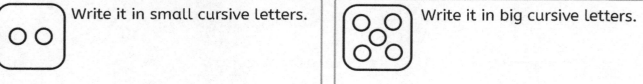

are   eating   house   made   love

call   game   hope   only   nut

⚀ Write it in all small letters.	⚃ Write it in all big letters.
⚁ Write it in small cursive letters.	⚄ Write it in big cursive letters.
⚂ Write it using fancy letters.	⚅ Write each letter in different colors.

Word Illustrations

Look at the picture and choose the spelling word that matches. Write the word in the box.

are	eating	house	made	love
call	game	hope	only	nut

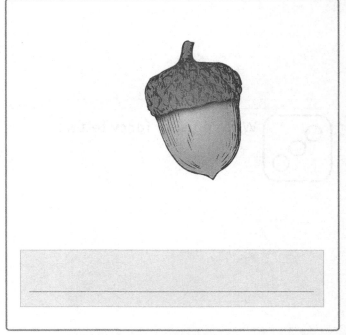

Spelling word boxes

Fill in the blank spaces with the missing letters.

are	eating	house	made	love
call	game	hope	only	nut

a □ □

g □ □ □

o □ □ □

l □ □ □

n □ □

m □ □ □

e □ □ □ □ □

Tracing spelling words

Trace your spelling words below using the tool at the top of each column.

pencil	crayon	marker
are	are	are
call	call	call
eating	eating	eating
game	game	game
house	house	house
hope	hope	hope
made	made	made
only	only	only
love	love	love
nut	nut	nut

Pattern block spelling

Use the pattern block spelling words to create real-life pattern block spelling words.

ARE	HOPE
CALL	MADE
EATING	ONLY
GAME	LOVE
HOUSE	NUT

Emoji spelling
Use the emoji code and write the word.

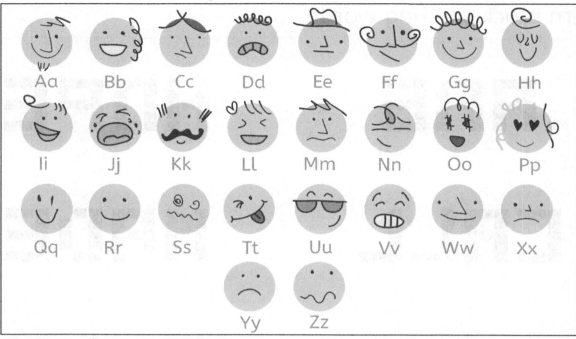

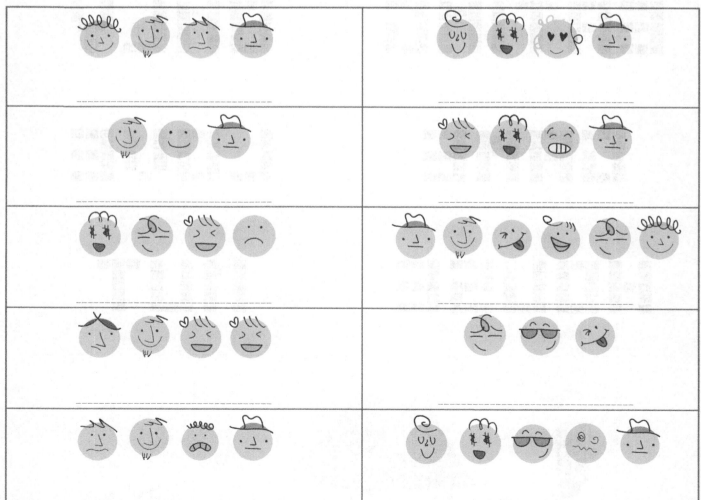

Spelling maze

Make your way through the maze. Check off your spelling words as you see them.

game	are
hope	only
call	made
eating	nut
house	love

Vowels & Consonants

Color all the vowels green and consonants orange in each of the spelling words!

are	hope
call	made
eating	only
game	love
house	nut

Spelling spiral

Write each spelling word on the spiral until you reach the middle.

game	are
hope	only
call	made
eating	nut
house	love

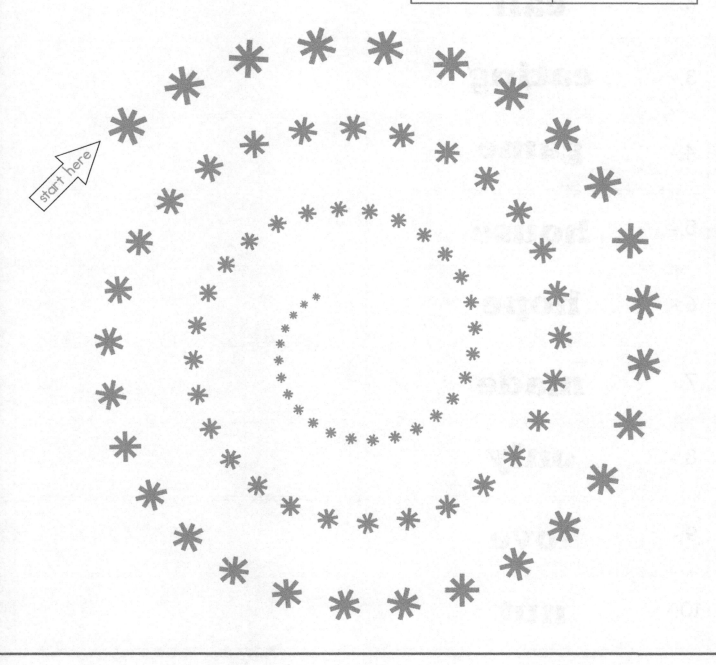

start here

Spelling rhymes

Can you think of a word that rhymes with each of your spelling words?

	spelling word	rhyming word
1.-	**are**	
2.-	**call**	
3.-	**eating**	
4.-	**game**	
5.-	**house**	
6.-	**hope**	
7.-	**made**	
8.-	**only**	
9.-	**love**	
10.-	**nut**	

Fun Spelling and Writing

Trace the word, write it upside down and with your eyes closed.

trace word	upside down	eyes closed
are		
call		
eating		
game		
house		
hope		
made		
only		
nut		
love		

Spelling words scramble

Unscramble the letters to write the correct words.

amed _____

mage _____

lcal _____

yonl _____

phoe _____

tangie _____

suoeh _____

call

eating

house

only

game

made

hope

Spin & spell

Spin the spinner and spell the word that correlates with the number spun!

call	4
house	3
are	10
eating	9
hope	7
game	5
love	1
only	8
made	2
nut	6

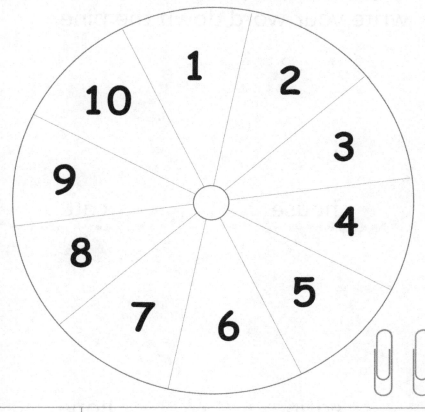

Pine tree spelling

Begin with the first letter and add one more letter as you write your word down the pine.

h
ho
hou
hous
house

call

nut

eating

hope

game

are

made

only

love

Spelling word syllables

Color the number of syllables for each of your spelling words.

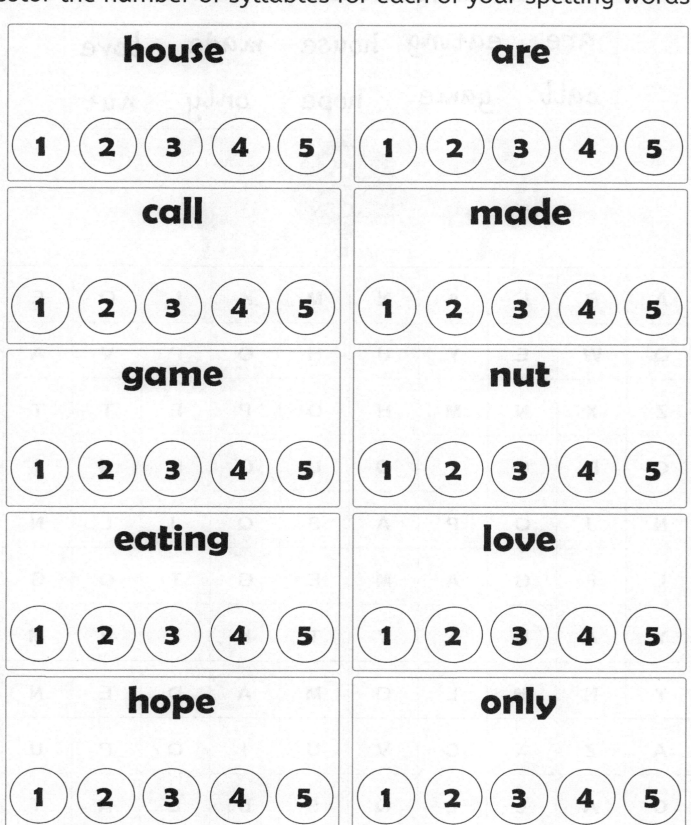

house
1 2 3 4 5

are
1 2 3 4 5

call
1 2 3 4 5

made
1 2 3 4 5

game
1 2 3 4 5

nut
1 2 3 4 5

eating
1 2 3 4 5

love
1 2 3 4 5

hope
1 2 3 4 5

only
1 2 3 4 5

Spelling word search

Find all the words to solve the word search.

are   eating   house   made   love
call   game   hope   only   nut

A	R	E	A	N	M	K	L	O	E
Q	W	E	Y	U	H	O	P	V	A
Z	X	N	M	H	O	P	E	T	T
O	D	U	I	O	U	G	B	N	I
N	J	O	P	A	S	Q	J	L	N
L	F	G	A	M	E	G	T	O	G
Y	A	B	I	Y	T	K	L	V	M
Y	N	M	L	O	M	A	D	E	N
A	Z	X	C	V	U	I	O	P	U
C	A	L	L	Q	S	D	E	R	T

Stamping Spelling Words

Read the word, then stamp or color each word as you go.

are	hope	call	house	eating
game	house	made	nut	only
only	are	game	eating	call
nut	hope	only	game	made
are	made	eating	hope	house
game	hope	call	nut	only

Spelling word art

Color in the fancy letters and decorate around each of the spelling words.

 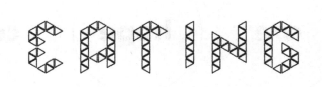

call

house

nut

hope

game

made

love

only

Spelling color

Trace and color each spelling word using the color code.

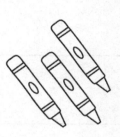

call	red	game	pink
house	green	love	grey
are	blue	only	brown
eating	orange	made	yellow
hope	purple	nut	black

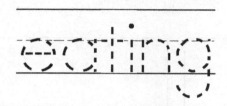

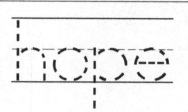

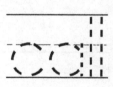

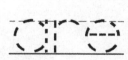

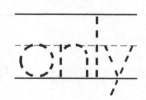

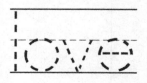

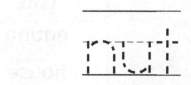

Spelling words rainbow

Write each spelling word under the rainbow.

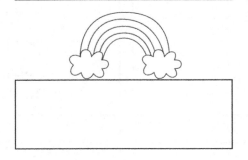

game	are
hope	only
call	made
eating	nut
house	love

Count & write

How many letters does the word have?

Spelling word		How many letters?
h-o-p-e	→	
l-o-v-e	→	
e-a-t-i-n-g	→	
g-a-m-e	→	
h-o-u-s-e	→	
a-r-e	→	
m-a-d-e	→	
o-n-l-y	→	
n-u-t	→	
c-a-l-l	→	

Write a sentence

Write a sentence using the spelling words found in the box. March each word after using it.

love call house are eating hope game only made nut

1.

2.

3.

4.

5.

6.

7.

8.

9.

10.

Word tile spelling

Add the sum of the letter tiles for each of your spelling words.

  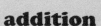

spelling word	addition	total
a₁ r₂ e₃	1+2+3=	6
c₃ a₂ l₁ l₁		
m₁ a₂ d₄ e₁		
g₄ a₂ m₃ e₁		
h₁ o₃ p₁ e₂		
h₁ o₄ u₂ s₃ e₄		
e₁ a₃ t₁ i₃ n₄ g₂		
n₁ u₂ t₃		
l₂ o₁ v₁ e₄		
o₁ n₂ l₃ y₂		

Create a story
Create a story with your spelling words.

love call house are eating hope game only made nut

Draw a picture of your story.

_____

_____

_____

_____

_____

_____

_____

SPELLING LIST

These are the words that the students will practice in this volume.

foot

night

rock

late

time

story

rain

tall

wash

black

Alphabetical kites

Write each word in ABC order on the given kites.

foot	rock	time	rain	wash
night	late	story	tall	black

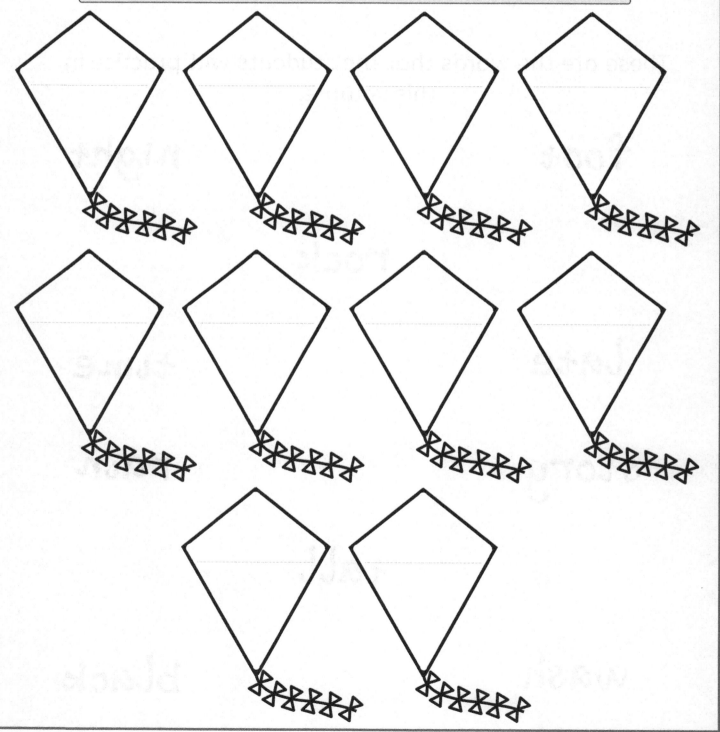

MAGIC Spelling Words

Write each word with white crayon and color over with marker to watch it "magically" appear.

foot	rock	time	rain	wash
night	late	story	tall	black

Secret code spelling words

Use the picture code to spell each of your words.

1.-

2.-

3.-

4.-

5.-

6.-

7.-

8.-

9.-

10.-

How many sounds?

Write the number of sounds in each of your spelling words.

spelling word	sounds
1.- rock	1 2 3 4 5
2.- night	1 2 3 4 5
3.- late	1 2 3 4 5
4.- foot	1 2 3 4 5
5.- time	1 2 3 4 5
6.- story	1 2 3 4 5
7.- rain	1 2 3 4 5
8.- black	1 2 3 4 5
9.- tall	1 2 3 4 5
10.- wash	1 2 3 4 5

Sign language spelling

Sign each of your spelling words. Mark them off as you go.

Aa	Bb	Cc	Dd	Ee	Ff	Gg	Hh	Ii
Jj	Kk	Ll	Mm	Nn	Oo	Pp	Qq	
Rr	Ss	Tt	Uu	Vv	Ww	Xx	Yy	Zz

foot	☐	rock	☐
rain	☐	black	☐
tall	☐	late	☐
time	☐	story	☐
wash	☐	night	☐

Roll a spelling word

Roll the dice then follow the directions for the number you rolled and complete the given task.

foot	rock	time	rain	wash
night	late	story	tall	black

Write it in all small letters.

Write it in all big letters.

Write it in small cursive letters.

Write it in big cursive letters.

Write it using fancy letters.

Write each letter in different colors.

Word Illustrations

Look at the picture and choose the spelling word that matches. Write the word in the box.

foot   rock   time   rain   wash

night   late   story   tall   black

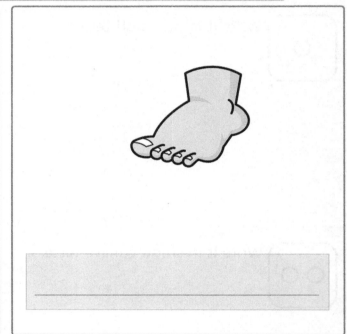

Spelling word boxes

Fill in the blank spaces with the missing letters.

foot   rock   time   rain   wash

night   late   story   tall   black

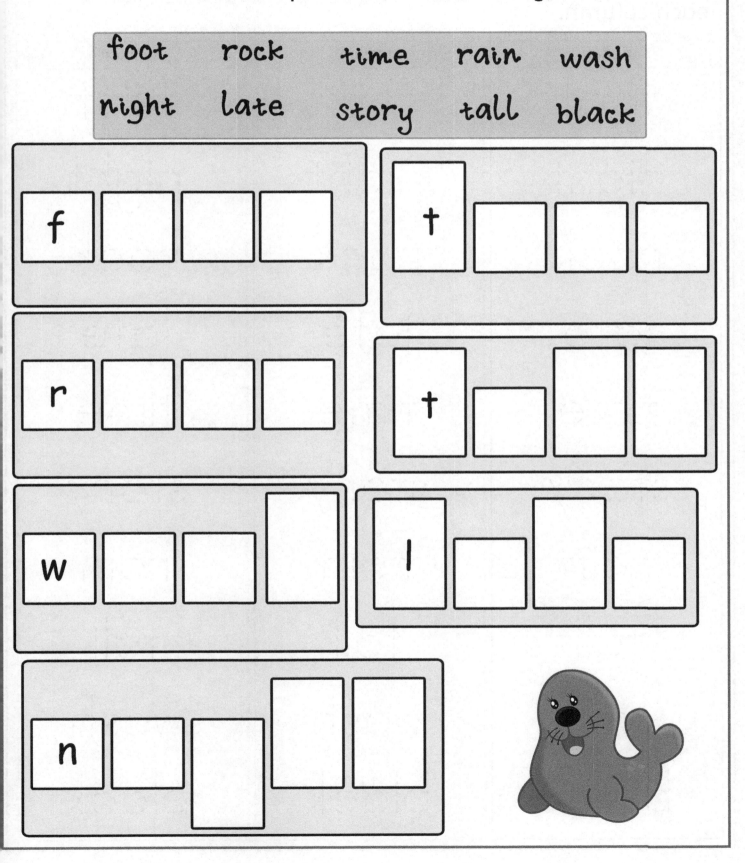

Tracing spelling words

Trace your spelling words below using the tool at the top of each column.

pencil	crayon	marker
foot	foot	foot
night	night	night
rock	rock	rock
late	late	late
time	time	time
story	story	story
rain	rain	rain
tall	tall	tall
wash	wash	wash
black	black	black

Pattern block spelling

Use the pattern block spelling words to create real-life pattern block spelling words.

STORY	TIME
RAIN	LATE
TALL	WASH
BLACK	FOOT
ROCK	NIGHT

Emoji spelling

Use the emoji code and write the word.

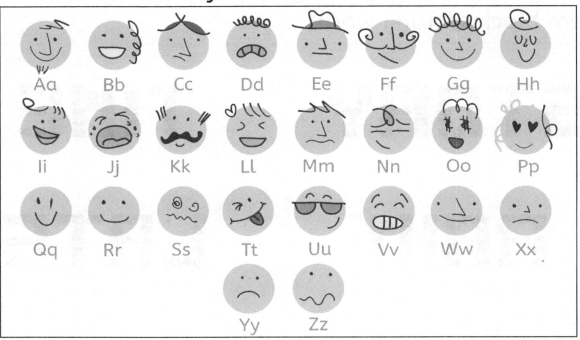

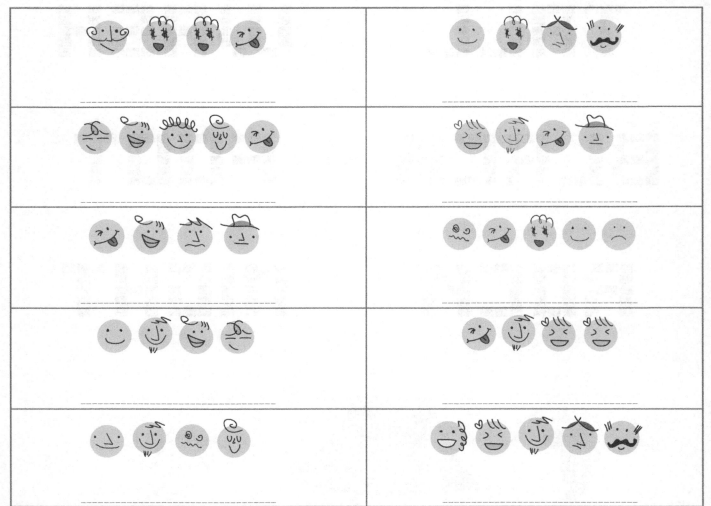

Spelling maze

Make your way through the maze. Check off your spelling words as you see them.

foot	story
time	rock
late	tall
night	black
rain	wash

Vowels & Consonants

Color all the vowels green and consonants orange in each of the spelling words!

time

rain

story

late

tall

wash

black

rock

foot

night

Spelling spiral

Write each spelling word on the spiral until you reach the middle.

tall	rock
black	late
wash	time
foot	story
night	rain

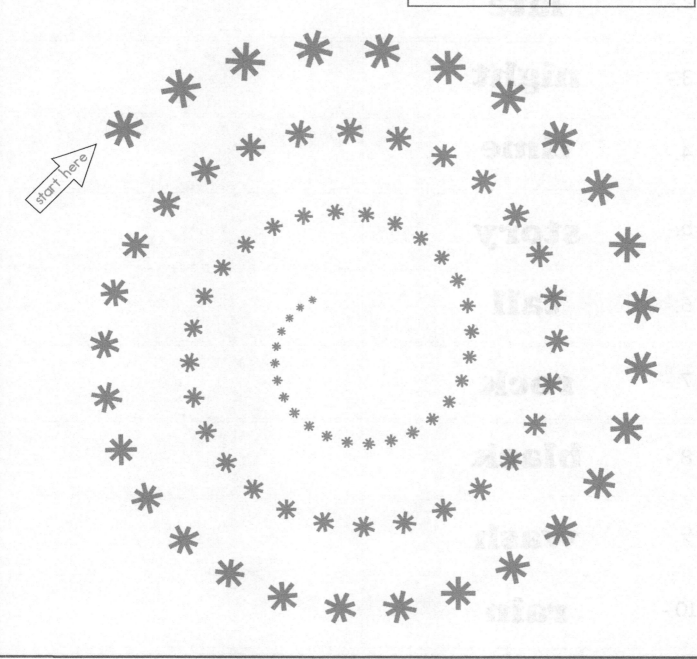

start here

Spelling rhymes

Can you think of a word that rhymes with each of your spelling words?

	spelling word	rhyming word
1.-	**foot**	
2.-	**late**	
3.-	**night**	
4.-	**time**	
5.-	**story**	
6.-	**tall**	
7.-	**rock**	
8.-	**black**	
9.-	**wash**	
10.-	**rain**	

Fun Spelling and Writing

Trace the word, write it upside down and with your eyes closed.

trace word	upside down	eyes closed
night		
story		
late		
rain		
tall		
rock		
wash		
foot		
black		
time		

Spelling words scramble

Unscramble the letters to write the correct words.

atel _____

otfo _____

lcbka _____

tryso _____

irna _____

gtinh _____

krco _____

foot

story

night

rock

late

rain

black

Spin & spell

Spin the spinner and spell the word that correlates with the number spun!

time	4
story	3
late	10
tall	9
rain	7
rock	5
black	1
foot	8
night	2
wash	6

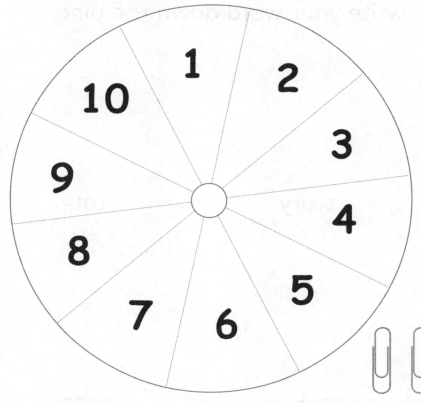

Pine tree spelling

Begin with the first letter and add one more letter as you write your word down the pine.

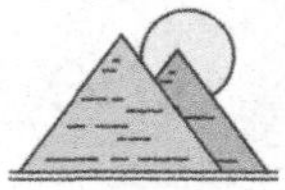

s
st
sto
stor
story

late

tall

rock

time

foot

night

rain

wash

black

Spelling word syllables

Color the number of syllables for each of your spelling words.

black

① ② ③ ④ ⑤

wash

① ② ③ ④ ⑤

tall

① ② ③ ④ ⑤

rain

① ② ③ ④ ⑤

story

① ② ③ ④ ⑤

rock

① ② ③ ④ ⑤

late

① ② ③ ④ ⑤

time

① ② ③ ④ ⑤

night

① ② ③ ④ ⑤

foot

① ② ③ ④ ⑤

Spelling word search

Find all the words to solve the word search.

foot   rock   time   rain   wash
night   late   story   tall   black

F	O	O	T	Q	W	E	D	F	F
A	Z	X	I	S	T	O	R	Y	P
U	J	K	M	G	B	W	A	S	H
B	R	Q	E	Z	B	X	I	C	V
N	R	T	A	L	L	R	N	Y	I
M	O	B	D	Z	A	V	F	B	P
U	C	N	F	A	C	T	R	L	L
K	K	M	C	Q	K	U	B	A	O
L	D	K	V	N	I	G	H	T	K
O	V	L	H	W	F	G	J	E	M

Stamping Spelling words

Read the word, then stamp or color each word as you go.

foot	rock	night	late	foot
time	story	foot	night	rock
rain	black	wash	tall	foot
story	late	rain	story	rock
night	black	rain	foot	late
black	rain	time	late	night

Spelling word art

Color in the fancy letters and decorate around each of the spelling words.

 wash

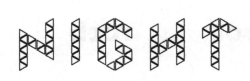 NIGHT

foot

time

late

rock

story

rain

tall

black

Spelling color

Trace and color each spelling word using the color code.

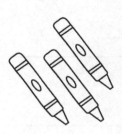

foot	red		late	pink
night	green		time	grey
rock	blue		story	brown
wash	orange		tall	yellow
black	purple		rain	black

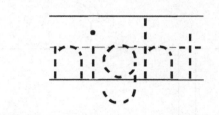

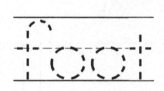

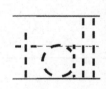

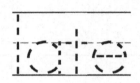

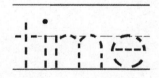

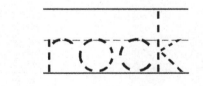

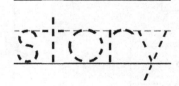

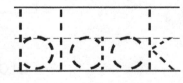

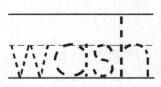

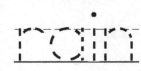

Spelling words rainbow

Write each spelling word under the rainbow.

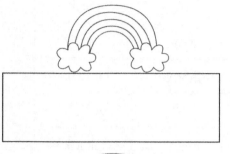

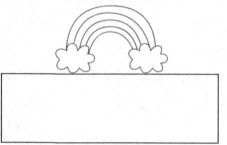
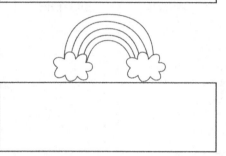
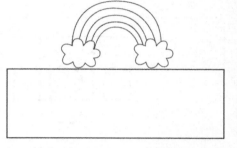

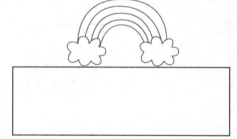

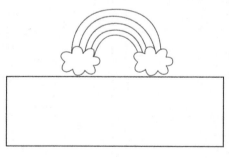

black	time
wash	story
black	late
foot	rock
rain	night

Count & write
How many letters does the word have?

Spelling word		How many letters?
n-i-g-h-t	→	
s-t-o-r-y	→	
l-a-t-e	→	
r-o-c-k	→	
f-o-o-t	→	
t-i-m-e	→	
r-a-i-n	→	
w-a-s-h	→	
b-l-a-c-k	→	
t-a-l-l	→	

Write a sentence

Write a sentence using the spelling words found in the box. March each word after using it.

foot tall night story late rock time rain wash black

1.

2.

3.

4.

5.

6.

7.

8.

9.

10.

Word tile spelling

Add the sum of the letter tiles for each of your spelling words.

spelling word	addition	total
$_4$f $_2$o $_3$o $_1$t	4+2+3+1=	10
$_1$t $_2$a $_4$l $_5$l		
$_1$r $_2$o $_5$c $_1$k		
$_2$w $_3$a $_3$s $_4$h		
$_1$r $_3$a $_4$i $_2$n		
$_1$n $_4$i $_2$g $_5$h $_4$t		
$_1$b $_2$l $_1$a $_3$c $_5$k		
$_5$s $_2$t $_1$o $_4$r $_3$y		
$_6$l $_1$a $_2$t $_4$e		
$_3$t $_2$i $_3$m $_1$e		

Create a story
Create a story with your spelling words.

foot tall night story late rock time rain wash black

Draw a picture of your story.

SPELLING LIST

These are the words that the students will practice in this volume.

week

happy

work

drive

start

miss

king

cut

duck

best

Alphabetical kites

Write each word in ABC order on the given kites.

week	work	start	king	best
happy	drive	miss	cut	duck

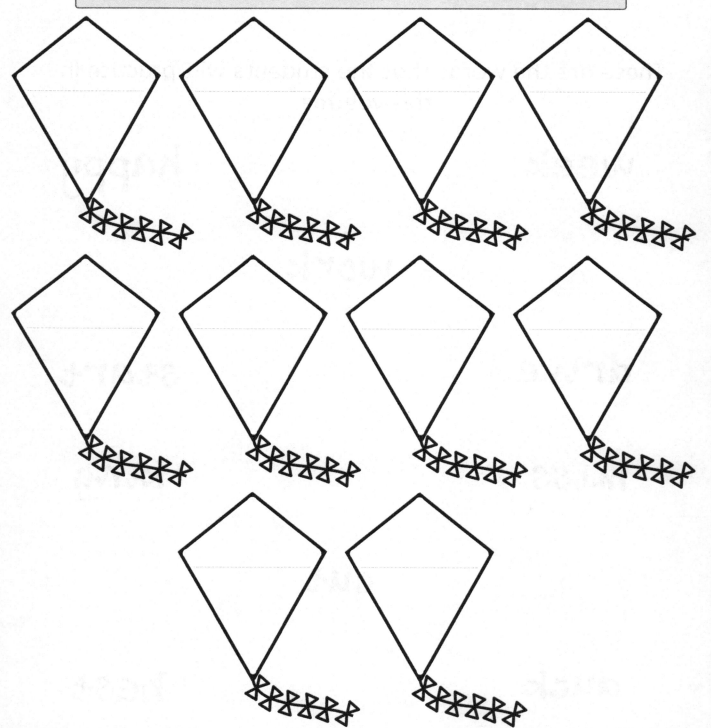

MAGIC Spelling Words

Write each word with white crayon and color over with marker to watch it "magically" appear.

week	work	start	king	best
happy	drive	miss	cut	duck

Secret code spelling words

Use the picture code to spell each of your words.

A	H	O	V
B	I	P	W
C	J	Q	X
D	K	R	Y
E	L	S	Z
F	M	T	
G	N	U	

1.- _BEST_

2.- _CUT_

3.- _KING_

4.- _START_

5.- _WEEK_

6.- _DUCK_

7.- _MISS_

8.- _DRIVE_

9.- _WORK_

10.- _HAPPY_

How many sounds?

Write the number of sounds in each of your spelling words.

spelling word	sounds
1.- week	1 2 3 4 5
2.- work	1 2 3 4 5
3.- start	1 2 3 4 5
4.- king	1 2 3 4 5
5.- best	1 2 3 4 5
6.- happy	1 2 3 4 5
7.- drive	1 2 3 4 5
8.- miss	1 2 3 4 5
9.- cut	1 2 3 4 5
10.- duck	1 2 3 4 5

Sign language spelling
Sign each of your spelling words. Mark them off as you go.

happy ☐	miss ☐
work ☐	king ☐
week ☐	cut ☐
drive ☐	duck ☐
start ☐	best ☐

 # Roll a spelling word

Roll the dice then follow the directions for the number you rolled and complete the given task.

week	work	start	king	best
happy	drive	miss	cut	duck

Write it in all small letters.

Write it in all big letters.

 Write it in small cursive letters.

Write it in big cursive letters.

Write it using fancy letters.

 Write each letter in different colors.

Word Illustrations

Look at the picture and choose the spelling word that matches. Write the word in the box.

week	work	start	king	best
happy	drive	miss	cut	duck

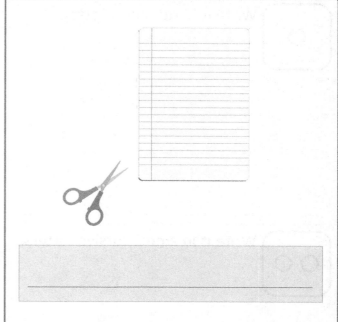

Spelling word boxes

Fill in the blank spaces with the missing letters.

week   work   start   king   best

happy   drive   miss   cut   duck

| w | | | |

| d | | | |

| m | | | |

| k | | | |

| w | | | |

| c | | |

| h | | | | |

Tracing spelling words

Trace your spelling words below using the tool at the top of each column.

pencil	crayon	marker
week	week	week
happy	happy	happy
work	work	work
drive	drive	drive
start	start	start
miss	miss	miss
king	king	king
cut	cut	cut
duck	duck	duck
best	best	best

Pattern block spelling

Use the pattern block spelling words to create real-life pattern block spelling words.

DRIVE	MISS
KING	CUT
DUCK	START
BEST	WORK
WEEK	HAPPY

Emoji spelling
Use the emoji code and write the word.

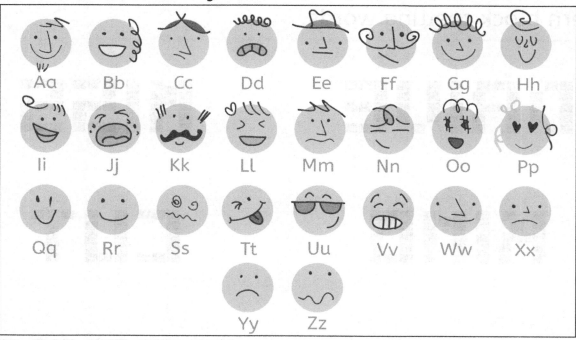

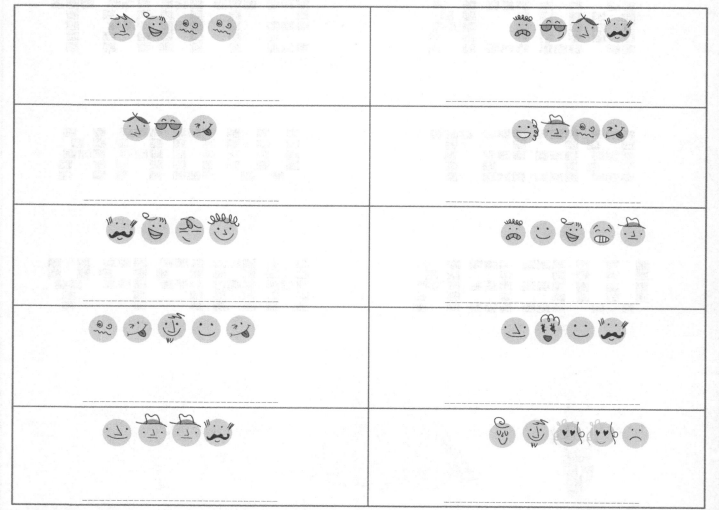

Spelling maze

Make your way through the maze. Check off your spelling words as you see them.

week	drive
miss	work
duck	cut
happy	start
king	best

Vowels & Consonants

Color all the vowels green and consonants orange in each of the spelling words!

start

duck

king

best

cut

week

miss

work

drive

happy

Spelling spiral

Write each spelling word on the spiral until you reach the middle.

week	start
work	king
happy	duck
drive	best
miss	cut

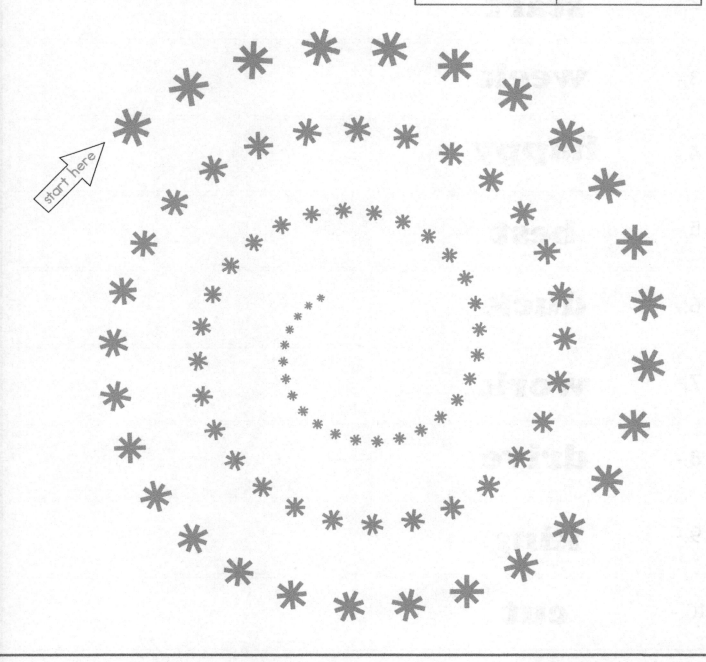

start here

Spelling rhymes

Can you think of a word that rhymes with each of your spelling words?

	spelling word	rhyming word
1.-	**miss**	
2.-	**start**	
3.-	**week**	
4.-	**happy**	
5.-	**best**	
6.-	**duck**	
7.-	**work**	
8.-	**drive**	
9.-	**king**	
10.-	**cut**	

Fun Spelling and Writing

Trace the word, write it upside down and with your eyes closed.

trace word	upside down	eyes closed
duck		
cut		
miss		
drive		
happy		
week		
work		
start		
king		
best		

Spelling words scramble

Unscramble the letters to write the correct words.

etbs _____

ikgn _____

pahyp _____

uct _____

atrst _____

cdku _____

iderv _____

happy

drive

duck

start

best

cut

king

Spin & spell

Spin the spinner and spell the word that correlates with the number spun!

start	4
miss	3
king	10
cut	9
best	7
duck	5
work	1
drive	8
week	2
happy	6

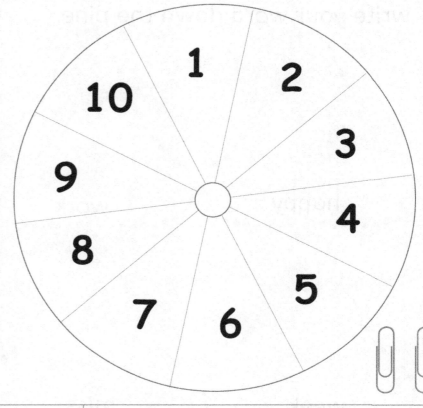

Pine tree spelling

Begin with the first letter and add one more letter as you write your word down the pine.

h
ha
hap
happ
happy

work

drive

week

miss

start

cut

king

best

duck

Spelling word syllables

Color the number of syllables for each of your spelling words.

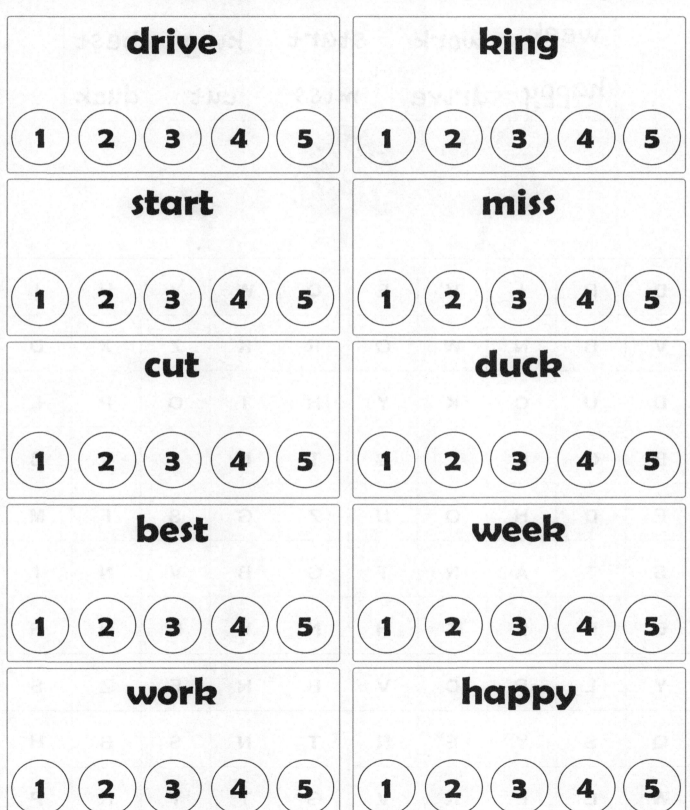

drive
1 2 3 4 5

king
1 2 3 4 5

start
1 2 3 4 5

miss
1 2 3 4 5

cut
1 2 3 4 5

duck
1 2 3 4 5

best
1 2 3 4 5

week
1 2 3 4 5

work
1 2 3 4 5

happy
1 2 3 4 5

Spelling word search

Find all the words to solve the word search.

week　　work　　start　　king　　best

happy　　drive　　miss　　cut　　duck

D	R	I	V	E	Q	W	Y	U	I
V	B	N	W	O	R	K	Z	X	D
D	U	C	K	Y	H	I	O	P	L
B	G	K	L	C	T	N	F	V	B
E	D	H	Q	U	Z	G	S	F	M
S	T	A	R	T	G	B	V	N	I
U	K	P	T	H	N	V	B	U	S
Y	L	P	C	V	B	N	E	Z	S
Q	S	Y	E	R	T	N	S	B	H
W	E	E	K	V	G	T	T	K	P

Stamping Spelling Words

Read the word, then stamp or color each word as you go.

week	happy	work	drive	start
miss	cut	king	best	duck
king	week	start	drive	miss
cut	drive	happy	work	duck
king	drive	miss	happy	week
start	work	best	duck	cut

Spelling word art

Color in the fancy letters and decorate around each of the spelling words.

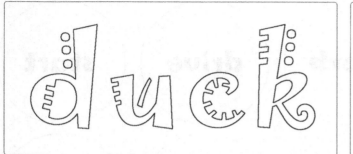 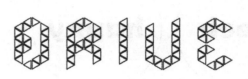

duck

DRIVE

cut

week

best

miss

king

start

work

happy

Spelling color

Trace and color each spelling word using the color code.

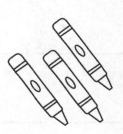

cut	red		miss	pink
work	green		week	grey
duck	blue		happy	brown
best	orange		start	yellow
drive	purple		work	black

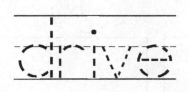
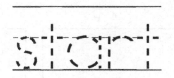

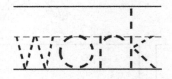
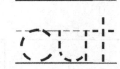

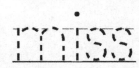
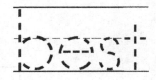

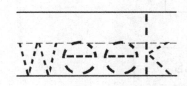
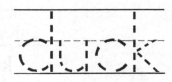

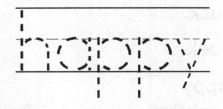
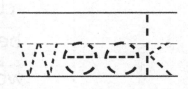

Spelling words rainbow

Write each spelling word under the rainbow.

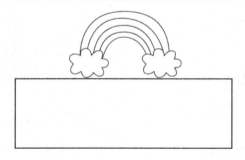

king	miss
start	drive
cut	duck
best	week
work	happy

Count & write

How many letters does the word have?

Spelling word		How many letters?
d-r-i-v-e	➡️	
m-i-s-s	➡️	
d-u-c-k	➡️	
w-e-e-k	➡️	
h-a-p-p-y	➡️	
w-o-r-k	➡️	
s-t-a-r-t	➡️	
k-i-n-g	➡️	
c-u-t	➡️	
b-e-s-t	➡️	

Write a sentence

Write a sentence using the spelling words found in the box.
March each word after using it.

week work happy stort miss drive king cut duck best

1.

2.

3.

4.

5.

6.

7.

8.

9.

10.

Word tile spelling
Add the sum of the letter tiles for each of your spelling words.

spelling word	addition	total
$_3$d $_1$u $_5$c $_1$k	3+1+5+1=	10
$_3$b $_4$e $_4$s $_1$t		
$_5$m $_1$i $_4$s $_2$s		
$_2$c $_1$u $_3$t		
$_2$k $_1$i $_1$n $_2$g		
$_1$d $_5$r $_3$i $_1$v $_4$e		
$_2$s $_3$t $_1$a $_1$r $_2$t		
$_4$h $_2$a $_3$p $_2$p $_1$y		
$_5$w $_3$e $_1$e $_2$k		
$_4$w $_1$o $_2$r $_3$k		

Create a story
Create a story with your spelling words.

week work happy stort miss drive king cut duck best

Draw a picture of your story.

Spelling word chain

Write and make a chain of spelling words.

eating		
rock		
happy		
work		
late		
only		
hope		
game		

Spelling word chain

Write and make a chain of spelling words.

are

love

wash

king

start

house

night

duck

Color by spelling word

Color the picture using the color code of spelling words.

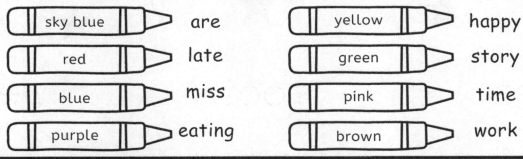

sky blue — are
red — late
blue — miss
purple — eating

yellow — happy
green — story
pink — time
brown — work

Trace Spelling Words

Trace and read spelling words.

are	foot	week
call	night	drive
eating	rock	happy
game	late	start
house	time	miss
hope	story	king
made	rain	cut
only	tall	best
love	wash	duck
nut	black	work

Find the hidden sounds

Match the hidden phoneme or sound that is missing in the spelling word.

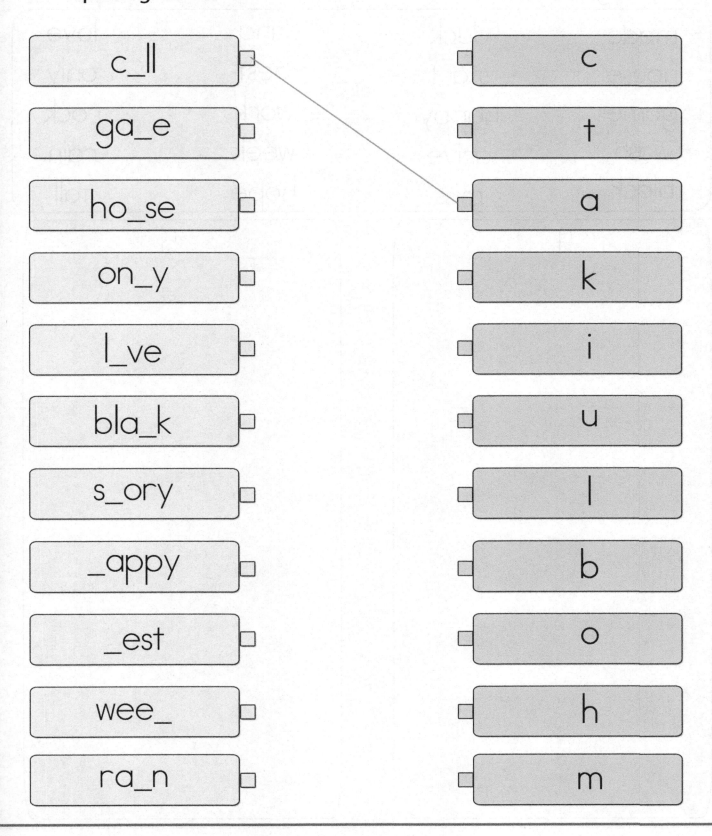

c_ll	c
ga_e	t
ho_se	a
on_y	k
l_ve	i
bla_k	u
s_ory	l
_appy	b
_est	o
wee_	h
ra_n	m

Find & count the sounds

Look at the words below. Count the sounds in each word and write it in the given boxes.

made	duck	king	love
house	start	best	only
game	happy	work	rock
wash	drive	week	rain
black	miss	hope	tall

4

made

5

Color spelling words

Read the word and color it according to the given color code.

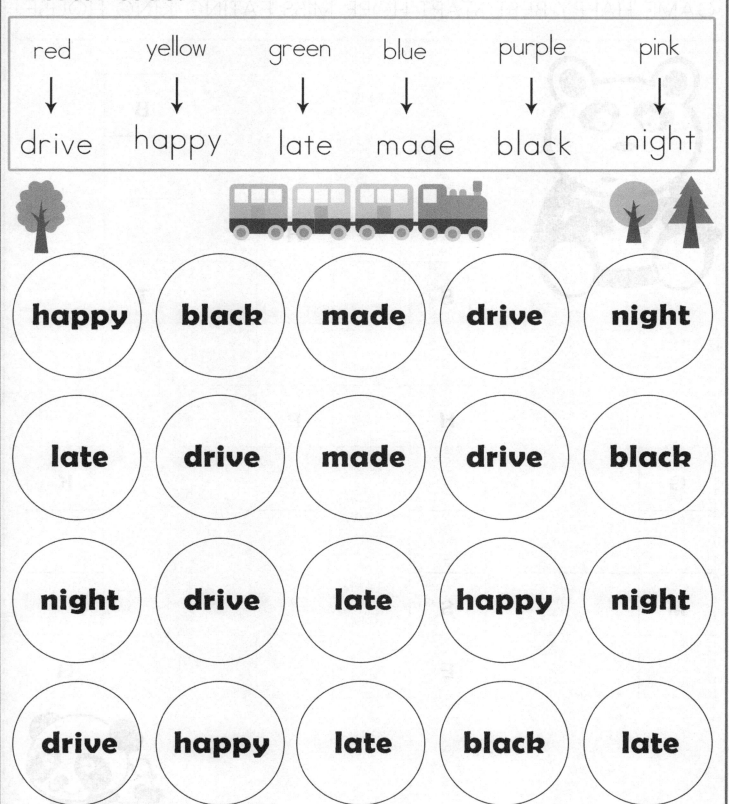

red	yellow	green	blue	purple	pink
↓	↓	↓	↓	↓	↓
drive	happy	late	made	black	night

happy	black	made	drive	night
late	drive	made	drive	black
night	drive	late	happy	night
drive	happy	late	black	late

Spelling crossword

Solve the crossword puzzle.

GAME HAPPY BEST START HOPE MISS EATING KING HOUSE

Trace & Match Spelling Words

Trace and match spelling words.

love	foot
black	rock
foot	house
made	week
work	drive
rock	happy
start	start
duck	made
house	love
happy	time
best	miss
week	king
drive	cut
cut	best
time	duck
king	work
miss	black

Create a story
Create a story with your spelling words.

game house made rock rain wash happy duck king

Draw a picture of your story.

85098367R00057